EXHIBIT 1

GARSDEN COMPANY

Balance Sheet
as of December 31, 2002
($000 omitted)

ASSETS		LIABILITIES AND EQUITY	
CURRENT ASSETS		**CURRENT LIABILITIES**	
Cash..	$ 1,449	Accounts payable..............................	$ 5,602
Marketable securities	246	Bank loan payable............................	1,000
Accounts receivable, net....................	9,944	Accrued liabilities............................	876
Inventories..	10,623	Estimated tax liability.......................	1,541
Prepaid expenses.............................	389	Current portion of long-term debt	500
Total current assets	22,651	Total current liabilities....................	9,519
NONCURRENT ASSETS		**NONCURRENT LIABILITIES**	
Property, plant, equipment at cost	$26,946	Long-term debt, less current portion	2,000
Accumulated depreciation..............	–13,534	Deferred income taxes....................	824
Property, plant, equipment, net..........	13,412		
Investments	1,110	Total liabilities	12,343
Patents and trademarks	403		
Goodwill	663	**EQUITY**	
		Common stock	1,000
		Additional paid-in capital	11,256
		Total paid-in capital........................	12,256
		Retained earnings.............................	13,640
		Total equity	25,896
TOTAL ASSETS.................................	$38,239	TOTAL LIABILITIES AND EQUITY	$38,239

EXHIBIT 2

GLENDALE MARKET

	Assets			Liabilities and Equity	
January 2. Glendale Market received $10,000 from John Smith and banked the money.	Cash................................	$10,000	Paid-in capital..................		$10,000
		$10,000			$10,000
January 3. Glendale Market borrowed $5,000 from a bank, giving a note therefor.	Cash................................	$15,000	Note payable.................... Paid-in capital..................		$ 5,000 10,000
		$15,000			$15,000
January 4. Glendale Market purchased inventory costing $2,000, paying cash for it.	Cash................................ Inventory	$13,000 2,000	Note payable.................... Paid-in capital..................		$ 5,000 10,000
		$15,000			$15,000
January 5. Glendale Market sold merchandise for $300 cash that cost $200.	Cash................................ Inventory	$13,300 1,800	Note payable.................... Paid-in capital.................. Retained earnings		$ 5,000 10,000 100
		$15,100			$15,100
January 6. Glendale Market purchased and received merchandise for $2,000, agreeing to pay within 30 days.	Cash................................ Inventory	$13,300 3,800	Accounts payable .... Note payable.................... Paid-in capital.................. Retained earnings		$ 2,000 5,000 10,000 100
		$17,100			$17,100
January 7. Merchandise costing $500 was sold for $800, which was received in cash.	Cash................................ Inventory	$14,100 3,300	Accounts payable .... Note payable.................... Paid-in capital.................. Retained earnings		$ 2,000 5,000 10,000 400
		$17,400			$17,400
January 8. Merchandise costing $600 was sold for $900, the customer agreeing to pay $900 within 30 days.	Cash................................ Accounts receivable .... Inventory	$14,100 900 2,700	Accounts payable .... Note payable.................... Paid-in capital.................. Retained earnings		$ 2,000 5,000 10,000 700
		$17,700			$17,700

EXHIBIT 3

ACCOUNTS FOR GREEN COMPANY

Assets	Liabilities and Equity

Cash

(Dr.)	(Cr.)
Beg. bal. 1,000	

Accounts Receivable

(Dr.)	(Cr.)
Beg. bal. 3,000	

Inventory

(Dr.)	(Cr.)
Beg. bal. 4,000	

Other Assets

(Dr.)	(Cr.)
Beg. bal. 10,000	

Accounts Payable

(Dr.)	(Cr.)
	2,000 Beg. bal.

Paid-in Capital

(Dr.)	(Cr.)
	7,000 Beg. bal.

Retained Earnings

(Dr.)	(Cr.)
	9,000 Beg. bal.

EXHIBIT 4

GLENDALE MARKET
JOURNAL

2002		Accounts		Dr.	Cr.
Jan.	2	Cash	√	10,000	
		Paid-in Capital	√		10,000
	3	Cash	√	5,000	
		Notes Payable	√		5,000
	4	Inventory	√	2,000	
		Cash	√		2,000
	5	Cash	√	300	
		Revenues	√		300
	5	Expenses	√	200	
		Inventory	√		200
	6	Inventory	√	2,000	
		Accounts Payable	√		2,000
	7	Cash	√	800	
		Revenues	√		800
	7	Expenses	√	500	
		Inventory	√		500
	8				
	8				

EXHIBIT 4 (continued)

GLENDALE MARKET
JOURNAL

20 _ _		Transactions		Dr.	Cr.

EXHIBIT 5

GLENDALE MARKET LEDGER

Cash	
10,000	2,000
5,000	
300	
800	

Accounts Payable	
	2,000

Revenues	
	300
	800

Accounts Receivable	

Note Payable	
	5,000

Expenses	
200	
500	

Inventory	
2,000	200
2,000	500

Paid-in Capital	
	10,000

Retained Earnings	

EXHIBIT 6 FINANCIAL STATEMENTS

GLENDALE MARKET
Balance Sheet as of January 8

Assets		Liabilities and Equity	
Cash	$14,100	Accounts payable	$
Accounts receivable		Note payable	
Inventory		Paid-in capital	
		Retained earnings	
Total Assets	$	Total Liabilities and Equity......	$

Income Statement
for the period January 2–8

Revenues	$
Expenses..................................	
Net Income..............................	$

EXHIBIT 7

TRANSACTIONS OF HOMES, INC.

Date	Event	Effects on Cash
May 2	Able agrees to buy House A from Homes, Inc., and makes a $16,000 down payment.	increase $16,000
May 15	Homes, Inc., pays $800 commission to the salesperson who sold House A (5% of cash received).	decrease $800
May	Homes, Inc., general expenses for May were $4,400 (assume for simplicity these were paid in cash in May).	decrease $4,400
June 2	Baker agrees to buy House B and makes a $24,000 down payment.	increase $24,000
June 5	Able completes the purchase of House A, paying $144,000 cash. Homes, Inc., delivers the deed to Able thereby delivering ownership of the house. (House A cost Homes, Inc., $140,000.)	increase $144,000
June 30	Homes, Inc., pays $1,200 commission to the salesperson who sold House B.	decrease $1,200
June	Homes, Inc., general expenses for June were $4,000.	decrease $4,000
July 2	Homes, Inc., pays $7,200 additional commission to the salesperson who sold House A.	decrease $7,200
July 3	Baker completes the purchase of House B, paying $216,000 cash. Homes, Inc., delivers the deed to Baker, thereby delivering ownership of the house. (House B cost Homes, Inc., $200,000.)	increase $216,000
July 30	Homes, Inc., pays $10,800 commission to the salesperson who sold House B.	decrease $10,800
July	Homes, Inc., general expenses for July were $4,800.	decrease $4,800

EXHIBIT 8

A "PACKAGE" OF ACCOUNTING REPORTS
($000 omitted)

GARSDEN COMPANY

Condensed Balance Sheet as of December 31, 2001

Assets

Current assets	$23,024
Buildings and equipment	14,100
Other assets	1,662
Total Assets	$38,786

Liabilities and Equity

Liabilities	$14,622
Equity:	
Paid-in capital	12,256
Retained earnings	11,908
Total Liabilities and Equity	$38,786

Condensed Balance Sheet as of December 31, 2002

Assets

Current assets	$22,651
Buildings and equipment	13,412
Other assets	2,176
Total Assets	$38,239

Liabilities and Equity

Liabilities	$12,343
Equity:	
Paid-in capital	12,256
Retained earnings	13,640
Total Liabilities and Equity	$38,239

Income Statement for the Year 2002

Sales revenue	$75,478
Less cost of sales	52,227
Gross margin	23,251
Less operating expenses	10,785
Income before taxes	12,466
Provision for income taxes	6,344
Net income	$ 6,122

Statement of Retained Earnings

Retained earnings, 12/31/01	$11,908
Add net income, 2002	6,122
	18,030
Less dividends	4,390
Retained earnings, 12/31/02	$13,640

EXHIBIT 9

LEWIS FUEL COMPANY

	Units	Unit Cost	Total Cost
Beginning inventory, April 1	400	1.00	
Purchase, April 10	300	1.10	
Purchase, April 20	300	1.20	
Total goods available			
Ending inventory, April 30	600		
Cost of sales, April			

FIFO Method

Goods Available .... $_____

Ending inventory:

_____ units @ $_____ = $_____

_____ units @ $_____ =   _____

Total 600 units....................................   _____

   Cost of sales ....   _____

LIFO Method

Goods Available .... $_____

Ending inventory:

_____ units @ $_____ = $_____

_____ units @ $_____ =   _____

Total 600 units....................................   _____

   Cost of sales ....   _____

Average-Cost Method

Average cost of $_____ / _____ = _____ cost per unit

Goods available $1,090

   Ending inventory 600 units @ $ _____ = _____

   Cost of sales   400 units @ $ _____ = _____

EXHIBIT 10

ARLEN COMPANY
Balance Sheets
($000 Omitted)

Assets

		As of December 31	
		2002	2001
Current assets			
Cash..		$ 20	$ 7
Accounts receivable....................................		40	42
Inventory..		60	56
Prepaid Expenses.......................................		20	20
Total current assets...............................		140	125
Noncurrent assets			
Land		$ 30	$ 30
Plant, at cost..	$120		$108
Less accumulated depreciation.................	70	50	64	44
Goodwill and patents		10	10
Total assets..		230	209

Liabilities and Equity

		2002	2001
Current liabilities			
Accounts payable.......................................		$ 30	$ 33
Accrued wages...		10	6
Income taxes payable.................................		20	20
Total current liabilities...........................		60	59
Noncurrent liabilities			
Mortgage bonds payable.............................		$ 40	$ 34
Total liabilities......................................		100	93
Shareholder equity			
Paid-in capital (4,800 shares outstanding)...........................		$ 60	$ 60
Retained earnings.......................................		$ 70	56
Total shareholder equity		130	116
Total Liabilities and Equity.....................		230	209

Income Statement, 2002
($000 Omitted)

		Percentage
Sales revenue..	$300	100.0
Less cost of sales	− 180	60.0
Gross margin	120	40.0
Less depreciation expense	− 6	2.0
other expenses	− 72	24.0
Earnings before interest and taxes	42	14.0
Interest expense	− 5	1.7
Earnings before income tax	37	12.3
Provision for income taxes......................	− 13	4.3
Net income	24	8.0
Less dividends	− 10	
Addition to equity	14	

EXHIBIT 11

ARLEN COMPANY
Statement of Cash Flows, 2002

Cash Flow from Operating Activities

Net income .... $ 24

Adjustments required to reconcile net income to cash flows:

Depreciation expense.. $ . . . .

Decrease in accounts receivable.............................. . . . .

Increase in inventory .... (. . . .)

Decrease in accounts payable.................................. (. . . .)

Increase in accrued wages ....

Total adjustments to net income ....

Total cash flow from operating expenses ....

Cash Flow from Investing Activities

Purchase of plant and property .... (. . . .)

Cash Flow from Financing Activities

Issuance of long-term debt... . . . .

Dividends paid .... (. . . .) (. . . .)

Net increase in cash and cash equivalents .... $ . . . .

Note: Parentheses indicate decreases in cash.

EXHIBIT 12

Report of Independent Auditors

The Board of Directors and Shareholders
Garsden Company

We have audited the accompanying balance sheets of Garsden Company as of December 31, 2002 and 2001, and the related statements of income and cash flows for each of the three years in the period ended December 31, 2002. These financial statements are the responsibility of the company's management. Our responsibility is to express an opinion on these financial statements based on our audits.

We conducted our audits in accordance with generally accepted auditing standards. Those standards require that we plan and perform the audit to obtain reasonable assurance about whether the financial statements are free of material misstatement. An audit includes examining, on a test basis, evidence supporting the amounts and disclosures in the financial statements. An audit also includes assessing the accounting principles used and significant estimates made by management, as well as evaluating the overall financial statement presentation. We believe that our audits provide a reasonable basis for our opinion.

In our opinion, the financial statements referred to above present fairly, in all material respects, the financial position of Garsden Company at December 31, 2002 and 2001, and the results of its operations and its cash flows for each of the three years in the period ended December 31, 2002, in conformity with generally accepted accounting principles.

Deane and Burnham

Boston, Massachusetts
February 21, 2003

EXHIBIT 13

ARLEN COMPANY
Factors Affecting Return on Equity
(Year 2002, $000 Omitted)

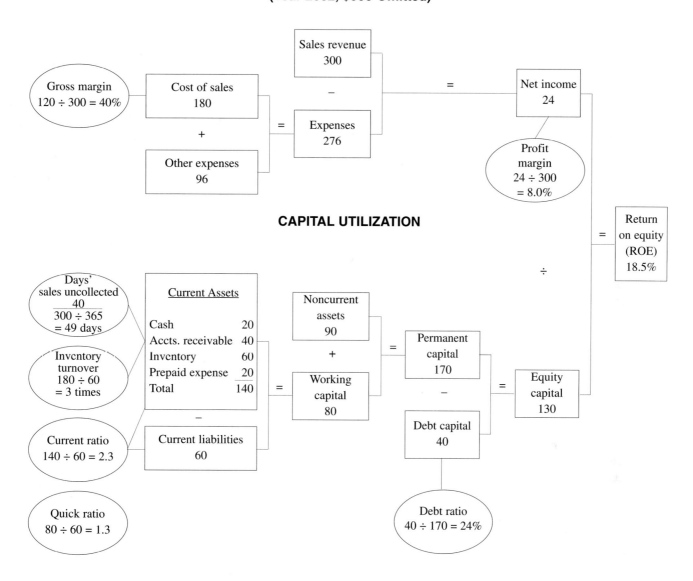

CAPITAL UTILIZATION

EXHIBIT 14

SOME COMMON RATIOS

Overall Performance	Numerator	Denominator
1. Return on equity (ROE)		
2. Earnings per share		
3. Price-earnings ratio		
4. Return on permanent capital		
Profitability		
5. Gross margin %		
6. Profit margin %		
7. EBIT margin %		
Capital utilization		
8. Days' sales uncollected		
9. Inventory turnover		
10. Current ratio		
11. Quick ratio		
12. Debt ratio		
13. Capital turnover		

EXHIBIT 15

Mercer Community Services
Statements of Financial Position
($000 Omitted)

Assets

	As of June 30	
	2002	2001
Assets:		
Cash and cash equivalents	$ 38	$ 230
Accounts receivable	1,065	835
Inventories	200	350
Prepaid Expenses	105	150
Contributions receivable	1,512	1,350
Land, buildings, and equipment	33,313	33,725
Long-term investments	109,035	101,750
Total assets	$145,268	$138,390

Liabilities and Net Assets

	2002	2001
Liabilities and Net Assets:		
Accounts payable	$ 1,285	$ 525
Refundable advances		325
Grants payable	438	650
Notes payable		570
Long-term debt	2,750	3,250
Total liabilities	4,473	5,320
Net assets:		
Unrestricted	57,614	51,835
Temporarily restricted	12,171	12,735
Permanently restricted	71,010	68,500
Total net assets	140,795	133,070
Total liabilities and net assets	$145,268	$138,390

Mercer Community Services
Statement of Activities
($000 Omitted)
Year Ended June 30, 2002

	Unrestricted	Temporarily Restricted	Permanently Restricted	Total
Revenues, gains and other support:				
Contributions	$4,320	$4,055	$140	$8,515
Fees	2,700			2,700
Income on long-term investments	2,800	1,290	60	4,150
Other investment income	425			425
Net realized and unrealized gains on				
long-term investments	4,114	1,476	2,310	7,900
Other	75			75
Net assets released from restrictions:				
Satisfaction of program restrictions	5,995	(5,995)		
Expiration of time restrictions	1,375	(1,375)		
Total revenue, gains, and other support	21,804	(549)	2,510	23,765
Expenses and losses:				
Program X	6,550			
Program Y	4,270			
Program Z	2,880			
Administration	1,250			
Fundraising	1,075			
Other losses		15		30
Total expenses	16,025	15		16,040
Change in net assets:	5,779	(564)	2,510	7,725
Net assets at beginning of year	51,835	12,735	68,500	133,070
Net assets at end of year	57,614	12,171	71,010	140,795

Post Tests

POST TEST 1

1. Give the accounting name for the following terms:

    (a) Things of value owned

        by an entity   _____.

    (b) Money   _____.

    (c) Claims of creditors   _____.

    (d) Claims of investors   _____.

2. List the two types of sources of funds; list first the type having the stronger claim on an entity's assets:

    Stronger claim _____

    Lesser claim   _____

3. A balance sheet reports the status of an entity . . . [at a point in time / over a period of time].

4. Give the fundamental accounting equation:

_____ = _____ + _____

5. The above equation is consistent with what concept?

_____-_____ _____

6. The money-measurement concept states that accounting reports only facts that can be expressed in _____ _____.

7. A balance sheet does not report all the facts about a business. What concept limits the amount or type of information that can be reported? _____-_____ _____

8. Brown Company has $10,000 cash. Fred Foy, its sole owner, withdraws $100 for his own use. Fred Foy is . . . [better off / worse off / no better or worse off] than he was before. Brown Company now has . . . [the same amount of / less] cash. The fact that this event affects Fred Foy differently than it affects Brown Company is an illustration of the _____ concept.

9. The entity concept states that accounts are kept for _____ as distinguished from the _____ who own those entities.

10. On December 31, 2001, Lewis Corporation has $12,000 cash on hand and in the bank. It owns other things of value, totaling $25,000. Its only debt is a bank loan of $10,000. Prepare a balance sheet for Lewis Corporation as of December 31, 2001, using the form below:

                _____ _____

      _____ _____ as of _____ _____ 2001

        _____   _____ and _____

_____ ....$_____   _____ ....$_____

Other _____ ...._____   _____ ...._____

_____ ....$_____   _____ ....$_____

11. The going-concern concept is: Accounting assumes that an _____ will continue to operate _____.

12. The asset-measurement concept is: If reliable information is available, accounting focuses on the _____ _____ of assets. Nonmonetary assets are reported at their original _____.

13. An item can be reported as an asset if it passes three of the following tests. Select "yes" for these and "no" for the others.

    (a) Item is valuable.   [yes / no]

    (b) Item is located in a building
        owned by the entity.   [yes / no]

    (c) Item is used by the entity.   [yes / no]

    (d) The entity has ordered the item. [yes / no]

    (e) Item was acquired at a
        measurable cost.   [yes / no]

    (f) Item is owned or controlled
        by the entity.   [yes / no]

14. Goodwill is a favorable name or reputation _____ by the entity.

15. An asset is classified as "current" if it is cash or is expected to be converted into cash in the near future, usually within _____ _____ [what time period?].

16. A liability is classified as "current" if it becomes due in the near future, usually within _____ _____ [what time period?].

17. Marketable securities are . . . [current / noncurrent] assets. Investments are . . . [current / noncurrent] assets.

18. Answer True or False:

    Shoes in a manufacturing company
    are considered inventory............................[T / F]

The building in which the shoes are manufactured is considered inventory................[T / F]

19. An insurance policy paid in advance of the time period covered is an example of a _____ _____.

20. A building, an item of equipment, and an automobile may all be examples of _____ and _____.

21. Parker Company operates a furniture store. On December 31, 2001, it had 30 desks that it was holding for sale. These would be reported as _____. The desk that is used by the president of Parker Company would be reported as _____ and _____.

22. Fox Company sold $1,000 of goods on credit to Golden Company. This would be recorded as an account . . . [receivable / payable] of Fox Company and as an account . . . [receivable / payable] of Golden Company.

23. Indicate whether the following statements about the balance sheet of a corporation are true or false:

    (a) Assets list all the valuable things
        owned by the entity............................[T / F]

    (b) The amount reported for the paid-in-
        capital item is approximately the
        fair value of the stock.........................[T / F]

    (c) The amount reported for total equity
        is approximately the fair value of the
        corporation's stock ....[T / F]

    (d) Total equities (also called "net worth")
        show approximately what the entity
        is worth..[T / F]

    (e) Retained earnings is the amount of
        cash retained in the entity ....[T / F]

Answers for Post Test 1 are on page 33.

POST TEST 2

1. On January 2, John Brown started the Brown Company. In January, Brown Company did the following things:

    (a) It received $5,000 cash from John Brown as its capital.

    (b) It borrowed $10,000 from a bank, giving a note therefor.

    (c) It purchased $4,000 of inventory for cash.

    (d) It sold $2,000 of its inventory for $6,000 to a customer, who paid $3,500 cash and agreed to pay $2,500 within 30 days.

    (e) It purchased an auto for $7,000. It paid $2,000 down and gave a note to the automobile dealer for the remaining $5,000.

    (f) Brown withdrew $1,000 cash for his personal use.

    (g) Brown was offered $10,000 for his equity in the business, but he refused the offer.

On a separate piece of paper, prepare a rough draft of a balance sheet for Brown Company as of the close of business January 31, and an income statement for January.

BROWN COMPANY

Balance Sheet as of _____ _____

_____			_____ and _____	
_____ ....$_____			_____ _____ ....$_____	
_____ _____ ...._____			_____-_____ _____ ...._____	
_____ ...._____			_____ _____ ...._____	
_____ ...._____			_____	
Total..$_____			Total...................................$_____	

BROWN COMPANY

Income Statement for _____

    _____ ....$_____

    _____ ....$_____

    Income..$_____

2. Brown Company's income was $4,000, but its Retained Earnings was only $3,000. Reread the first frame and choose the item (a–g) that explains the difference.

3. John Brown claims that the inventory as of January 31 is worth $6,000, as shown by the fact that inventory costing $2,000 was actually sold for $6,000. Would you change the balance sheet? . . . [Yes / No]. This is an illustration of the _____-_____ concept. Nonmonetary assets are reported at their _____ rather than their worth or _____ _____.

Answers for Post Test 2 are on page 34.

POST TEST 3

1. On March 5, Kay Company purchased $6,000 of inventory, paying cash. Prepare a journal entry for this transaction below.

Journal

2001	Transactions	Dr.	Cr.
___ __	_____	_____	
	_____		_____

2. On March 10, Kay Company made a $15,000 sale to a customer who paid $6,000 cash and agreed to pay the other $9,000 in 30 days. The merchandise sold had cost $8,000. Prepare a journal entry for the sale, below.

Journal

2001	Transactions	Dr.	Cr.
___ __	_____	_____	
	_____ _____		_____
	_____		_____

3. On March 10, Kay Company made a sale for $15,000 for merchandise that had cost $8,000. Prepare a journal entry to record the cost of the sale below.

Journal

2001	Transactions	Dr.	Cr.
___ __	_____		_____
	_____		_____

4. Recall from the previous frames that revenues from the sale on March 10 were $15,000 and that the merchandise sold had cost $8,000. Prepare the closing entries.

Journal

2001	Transactions	Dr.	Cr.
___ __	_____	_____	
	_____ _____		_____
___ __	_____ _____	_____
	_____		_____

5. The following journal entries will be used in Frames 6 and 7. There is no response required in this frame.

Journal

2001	Transactions	Dr.	Cr.
March 5	Inventory	6,000	
	Cash		6,000
March 10	Cash	6,000	
	Accounts Receivable	9,000	
	Revenues		15,000
March 10	Expenses	8,000	
	Inventory		8,000
March 31	Revenues	15,000	
	Retained Earnings		15,000
March 31	Retained Earnings	8,000	
	Expenses		8,000

6. Post the journal entries from the previous frame to the ledger accounts below.
Asset accounts:

Cash

Bal.	25,000	_____
	_____	
Bal.	_____	

Accounts Receivable

Bal.	11,000	
Bal.	_____	

Inventory

Bal.	40,000	_____
	_____	
Bal.	_____	

Property and Plant

Bal.	30,000	

7. Post the journal entries from Frame 5 to the ledger accounts below.

Liability and Equity accounts:

Accounts Payable
	16,000 Bal.

Paid-in Capital
	60,000 Bal.

Revenues
——	——

Expenses
——	——

Retained Earnings
——	30,000 Bal.
——	
	—— Bal.

8. Complete the following table by selecting Debits or Credits.

	Debits Credits
Increases in asset accounts are	[Dr. / Cr.]
Decreases in asset accounts are	[Dr. / Cr.]
Increases in liability accounts are	[Dr. / Cr.]
Decreases in liability accounts are	[Dr. / Cr.]
Increases in equity accounts are	[Dr. / Cr.]
Decreases in equity accounts are	[Dr. / Cr.]
Increases in revenue accounts are	[Dr. / Cr.]
Increases in expense accounts are	[Dr. / Cr.]

9. Refer back to Frames 6 and 7. Prepare a balance sheet for Kay Company as of March 31.

KAY COMPANY

Balance Sheet as of March 31

Assets		Liabilities and Equity	
Cash	$_____	Accounts payable	$_____
Accounts receivable	_____	Paid-in capital	_____
Inventory	_____	Retained earnings	_____
Property and Plant	_____		
Total	$_____	Total	$_____

10. Refer back to Frame 7. Prepare an income statement for Kay Company for March.

_____ _____

_____ _____ for _____

_____ .... $_____

_____ .... _____

_____ .... $_____

11. A critic said that the company had $25,000 cash at the beginning of March and $25,000 at the end of March, and since its cash balance was unchanged, it couldn't be said to have any income in March. This criticism is . . . [correct / incorrect].

12. The reason the criticism is incorrect is because income is an increase in _____ _____, not necessarily in _____. For example, the sales revenue of Kay Company in March was $15,000 and its income was $7,000 even though $9,000 was received in cash.

Answers for Post Test 3 are on pages 34 and 35.

POST TEST 4

1. The conservation concept states that increases in equity are recognized only when they are _____ _____, while decreases in equity are recognized as soon as they are _____ _____.

2. The materiality concept states: disregard _____ _____, but disclose all _____ _____.

3. What is the length of the usual accounting period? _____ _____. Financial statements prepared for shorter periods are called _____ statements.

4. Cash accounting reports items that increase or decrease cash. Accrual accounting reports items that change _____ or _____ _____, even though these changes may not affect cash.

5. Increases in equity associated with the entity's operations during a period are _____, and decreases are _____. The difference between them is labeled _____.

6. The realization concept states that revenues are recognized when goods or services are _____.

7. Hartwell Company manufactures a table in August and places it in its retail store in September. Ralph Smith, a customer, agrees to buy the table in October, it is delivered to him in November, and he pays the bill in December. In what month is the revenue recognized? _____

8. The receipt of cash is a debit to Cash. What is the offsetting credit and (type of account) for the following types of sales transactions?

Account credited
(a) Cash received prior to delivery

_____ ____ _____

(a _____)
(b) Cash received in same period as delivery

_____
(c) Cash received after the period of delivery

_____ _____

(an _____)

9. Similarly, revenue is a credit entry. What is the offsetting debit when revenue is recognized in each of these periods?

Account debited
(a) Revenue recognized prior to receipt of cash

_____ _____

(b) Revenue recognized in same period as receipt of cash

_____
(c) Revenue recognized in period following receipt of cash

_____ ____ _____

10. In February, Hartwell Company agrees to sell a table to a customer for $600, and the customer makes a down payment of $100 at that time. The cost of the table is $400. The table is delivered to the customer in March, and the customer pays the remaining $500 in April. Give the journal entries (if any) that would be made in February, March, and April for both the revenue and expense aspects of this transaction.

February

_____   _____

_____ ____ _____   _____

March

_____ _____   _____

_____ ____ _____   _____

_____   _____

March

_____   _____

_____   _____

April

_____   _____

_____ _____   _____

11. At the end of 2001, Maypo Company had accounts receivable of $200,000, and it estimated

that $2,000 of this amount was a bad debt. Its revenue in 2001, with no allowance for the bad debts, was $600,000.

(a) What account should be debited for the $2,000 bad debt? _____

(b) What account should be credited?

_____ ____ _____

_____

(c) What amount would be reported as *net* accounts receivable on the balance sheet? $_____

(d) What amount would be reported as revenue on the 1999 income statement? $_____

12. In 2002, the $2,000 of bad debt was written off.

(a) What account should be debited for this write off? _____ ____

_____ _____

(b) What account should be credited?

_____ _____

Answers for Post Test 4 are on pages 35 and 36.

POST TEST 5

1. An expenditure occurs in the period in which goods or services are . . . [acquired / consumed]. An expense occurs in the period in which goods or services are . . . [acquired / consumed].

2. A certain asset was acquired in May. There was therefore an _____ in May. At the end of May, the item was either on hand, or it was not. If it was on hand, it was an _____; if it was not on hand, it was an _____ in May.

3. Productive assets are . . . [expired / unexpired] costs. Expenses are . . . [expired / unexpired] costs.

4. The matching concept states that _____ associated with the revenues of a period are _____ of that period.

5. Expenses of a period consist of:

(a) _____ of the goods and services _____ during that period.

(b) Other _____ that benefit _____ of the period.

(c) _____

6. If Brown Company pays rent prior to the period that the rent covers, the amount is initially reported as a credit to cash and a debit to _____ Rent, which is a(n) . . . [asset / liability] account. If Brown Company pays rent after the period covered, the amount is initially recorded as a debit to Rent Expense and a credit to _____ Rent, which is a(n) . . . [asset / liability] account.

7. A brand new machine owned by Fay Company was destroyed by fire in 2001. It was uninsured. It had been purchased for $10,000 with the expectation that it would be useful for five years. The expense (i.e. loss) recorded in 2001 should be . . . [$2,000 / $10,000].

8. Gross margin is the difference between _____ _____ and _____ _____ _____ .

9. Give the numerator and denominator of the gross margin percentage:

_____ _____
_____
_____ _____

10. The difference between revenues and expenses in an accounting period (or the amount by which equity [i.e., retained earnings] increased from operating activities during the period) is called _____ _____ .

11. A distribution of earnings to shareholders is called _____ .

12. Give an equation that used the terms
(a) net income
(b) dividends
(c) retained earnings at the beginning of the period, and
(d) retained earnings at the end of the period.

( ) = ( ) + ( ) – ( )

Answers for Post Test 5 are on page 36.

POST TEST 6

1. A dealer sells a television set for $800 cash. It had cost $600. Write journal entries for the *four* accounts affected by this transaction.

Dr. _____   _____
    Cr. _____   _____
Dr. _____ _____ _____   _____
    Cr. _____   _____

2. When using the perpetual inventory method, a record is kept for _____ _____ , showing receipts, issues, and the amount on hand.

3. Write an equation that shows how the cost of sales is determined by deduction:

cost of sales = _____ _____
    + _____
    – _____ _____

4. Following is information about a certain product:

	Quantity	Unit Cost	Total Cost
Inventory, July 1	400	$1.00	$400
Purchases, July 15	200	$1.20	240
Total goods available	600		640
Inventory, July 31	300		

What was the cost of sales for July:

    (a) Under the FIFO method _____

    (b) Under the LIFO method _____

    (c) Under the average-cost method _____

5. In periods of inflation, many companies use the LIFO method in calculating their taxable income because LIFO gives a _____ cost of sales and hence a _____ taxable income.

6. A company discovers that the fair value of its inventory is $1,000 lower than its cost. What journal entry should it make?

Dr. _____ ____ _____   _____

   Cr. _____   _____

7. In a manufacturing business, what three elements enter into the cost of a manufactured item?

_____ _____, _____ _____, and _____.

8. Period costs become an expense during the period in which they were _____.

9. Product costs become an expense during the period in which the products were _____.

10. One type of overhead rate involves use of the total direct labor costs and total production overhead costs for a period. Write a ratio that shows how the overhead rate is calculated.

$$\frac{\text{Total } \underline{\hspace{2cm}} \underline{\hspace{1.5cm}} \text{ costs}}{\text{Total } \underline{\hspace{1.5cm}} \underline{\hspace{1.5cm}} \text{ costs}}$$

11. A given finished item requires $50 of direct materials and 5 hours of direct labor at $8 per hour. The overhead rate is $4 per direct labor hour. At what amount would the finished item be shown in inventory?

$_____ [= $_____ + $_____ + $_____]

12. An inventory turnover of 5 is generally . . . [better / worse] than an inventory turnover of 4 because it indicates that . . . [more / less] capital is tied up in inventory, and there is . . . [more / less] risk that the inventory will become obsolete.

Answers for Post Test 6 are on page 36.

POST TEST 7

1. The amount at which a new plant asset is recorded in the accounts includes its purchase price plus _____ _____ incurred to make the asset ready for its intended use (such as transportation and installation).

2. A plant asset is acquired in 2001. It is expected to be worn out at the end of 10 years and to become obsolete in five years. What is its service life? _____ years

3. Ordinarily, land . . . [is / is not] depreciated because its _____ _____ is indefinitely long.

4. A plant asset is acquired in 2001 at a cost of $20,000. Its estimated service life is 10 years, and its estimated residual value is $2,000:

    (a) The estimated depreciable cost of the asset is

       $ _____

(b) If the straight-line depreciation method is used, the depreciation rate for this asset is _____ percent.

(c) What amount will be recorded as depreciation expense in each year of the asset's life?

$_____

(d) What account will be debited and what account will be credited to record this depreciation expense?

Dr. _____ _____

Cr. _____ _____

(e) After five years have elapsed, how would this asset be reported on the balance sheet?

(1) _____ $_____

(2) _____ _____ _____ $_____

(3) _____ _____ $_____

5. A machine is purchased on January 2, 2001, for $20,000 and it has an expected life of five years and no estimated residual value.

(a) If the machine is still in use six years later, what amount of depreciation expense will be reported in for the sixth year? _____

(b) What amount, if any, will be reported on the balance sheet at the end of the sixth year?

[ ] (1) It will not be reported.

[ ] (2) It will be reported as follows:

_____ $_____

_____ _____ $_____

_____ _____ $_____

6. A machine is purchased on January 2, 2001, for $50,000. It has an expected service life of 10 years and no residual value. Eleven years later it is sold for $3,000 cash.

(a) There will be a . . . [loss / gain] of

$_____

(b) What account will be debited and what account credited to record this amount?

Dr. _____

Cr. _____ on _____ of _____

7. Give an example of each of the following types of assets, and give the name of the process used in writing off the cost of the second and third type.

Asset type	Example	Write-off process
Plant Asset	m_____ ,	Depreciation
	b_____	
Wasting asset	c_____ , o_____ _____	
	m_____	
Intangible asset	g_____ _____	
	t_____	

8. Conoil Company purchased a producing oil property for $10,000,000 on January 2, 2001. It estimated that the property contained one million barrels of oil and that the property had a service life of 20 years. In 2001, 40,000 barrels of oil were recovered from the property. What amount should be charged as an expense in 2001? $_____

9. Wasting assets and intangible assets are reported on the balance sheet in a different way than building, equipment, and similar plant assets. The difference is that wasting assets are reported at the _____ _____ and plant assets are reported at _____, _____ _____ , and _____ _____ .

10. In calculating its taxable income, a company tries to report its income as _____ as it can. In calculating its financial accounting income, a company tries to report its income as _____ as it can.

11. As compared with straight-line depreciation, accelerated depreciation writes off . . . [more / the same / less] depreciation in the early years of an asset's life and . . . [more / the same / less] in the later years. Over the whole life of the asset, accelerated depreciation writes off . . . [more / the same / less] total cost as straight-line depreciation.

12. Companies usually use accelerated depreciation in tax accounting because it . . . [increases / reduces] taxable income and hence income tax in the early years.

13. Assume an income tax rate of 40%. If a company calculated its financial accounting income (before income taxes) in 2001 as $6 million and its taxable income as $4 million, what amount would it report as income tax expense on its 2001 income statement? $_____

14. Fill in the missing name on the following table:

Income tax expense	$100,000
Income tax paid	−60,000
_____ _____ _____	$ 40,000

The $40,000 would be reported on the balance sheet as a(n) . . . [asset / liability].

Answers for Post Test 7 are on page 37.

POST TEST 8

1. The term working capital means the difference between _____ _____ and _____ _____ .

2. The two principal sources of a company's permanent capital are _____ and _____ .

3. Bonds obligate the company to make regular payments of _____ and _____ . Bonds are . . . [never / sometimes / always] current liabilities.

4. The two principal sources of equity capital are _____-____ _____ from _____ and _____ _____ (income not paid out as dividends).

5. A corporation issues 1,000 shares of $1 par value common stock in exchange for $10,000 cash. Complete the journal entry for this transaction:

Dr. Cash 10,000

   Cr. _____ _____ .... _____

      _____ ____-__ _____ .... _____

6. The equity section of a balance sheet is as follows:

Common stock (1,000 shares, no par value) $10,000

Other paid-in capital...20,000

Retained earnings...40,000

Total equity...$70,000

(a) The stated value per share is . . . [$10 / $30 / $70 / can't tell]

(b) The company received from its shareholders . . . [$10,000 / $30,000 / $70,000 / can't tell]

(c) The shareholders' equity is worth . . . [$10,000 / $30,000 / $70,000 / can't tell]

(d) The company has cash of at least . . . [$10,000 / $30,000 / $70,000 / can't tell]

(e) The company's income to date has totaled . . . [$40,000 / at least $40,000 / can't tell]

(f) If the company is liquidated, the shareholders will receive at least . . . [$10,000 / $30,000 / $70,000 / can't tell]

7. The dollar amount reported for common stock on the balance sheet is the amount for the number of shares . . . [authorized / issued]. This amount is called the amount _____ .

8. Kay Company had 200,000 shares of stock authorized. It issued 150,000 shares. It later bought back 10,000 shares. The 10,000 shares are called _____ stock. The total shareholder equity on the balance sheet would be the amount for _____ shares.

9. Preferred shareholders usually have preference as to _____ and also in the event of liquidation they have preference as to _____ _____.

10. A cash dividend . . . [increases / decreases / does not change] shareholder equity. A stock dividend . . . [increases / decreases / does not change] shareholder equity. A stock dividend . . . [increases / decreases / does not change] the number of shares of stock outstanding.

11. Select the correct words in the following table, which shows the principal differences between debt capital and equity capital.

	Bonds (Debt)	Stock (Equity)
Annual payments are required.	[Yes / No]	[Yes / No]
Principal payments are required.	[Yes / No]	[Yes / No]
Therefore, risk to the entity is	[Higher / Lower]	[Higher / Lower]
But its cost is relatively	[Higher / Lower]	[Higher / Lower]

12. Corcoran Company has the following permanent capital:

Debt capital ....$ 80,000

Equity capital 20,000

   Total $100,000

(a) Its debt ratio is _____%.

(b) The company is said to be highly _____.

13. Able Company owns 51 percent of the stock of Charlie Company, 50 percent of the stock of David Company, and 49 percent of the stock of Eastern Company. Able is the _____ company. The accounts of _____ _____ and _____ _____ would be consolidated in consolidated financial statements. The equity of the shareholders who own 49 percent of the stock of Charlie Company would be reported as the item _____ _____ on the consolidated balance sheet.

14. Able Company's income statement reported revenue of $1,000,000, of which $10,000 was sales to Charlie Company. Charlie Company's income statement reported revenue of $500,000, of which $20,000 was sales to Able Company. Revenue on the consolidated income statement would be reported as $_____.

Answers for Post Test 8 are on pages 37 and 38.

POST TEST 9

1. The preparation of a statement of cash flows is . . . [recommended / required] by U.S. accounting rules.

2. The income statement reports net income on a(n) _____ basis. The statement of cash flows adjusts net income to a(n) _____ basis.

3. The three sections of the statement of cash flows are:

   cash flow from _____ _____

   cash flow from _____ _____

   cash flow from _____ _____

4. At December 31, 2001, XYZ Corp. had accounts receivable of $70,000. At December 31, 2002, the company's accounts receivable balance was $65,000. This $5,000 decrease of accounts receivable . . . [decreased / had no effect on / increased] net income adjusted to a cash basis.

5. Accounts payable for XYZ Corp. decreased by $3,000 between December 31, 2001 and December 31, 2002. This change . . .[decreased / had no effect on / increased] net income adjusted to a cash basis.

6. The change in XYZ Corp.'s cash balance from the end of 2001 to the end of 2002 . . . [is / is not] part of the changes in current assets used to calculate "cash flow from operating activities."

7. XYZ Corp. had $2,000 in depreciation expense in 2002. This . . . [was / was not] a cash flow during that year.

8. To adjust XYZ Corp.'s net income to a cash basis, the $2,000 in depreciation expense should be . . . [added to net income / subtracted from net income / ignored].

9. Complete the "cash flow from operating activities" section of XYZ Corp.'s statement of cash flows. Assume accounts receivable decreased by $5,000, accounts payable decreased by $3,000, and depreciation expense was $2,000. There were no other changes in current assets.

Net income	$50,000
Depreciation expense	$_____
Decrease in accounts receivable	$_____
Decrease in accounts payable	($_____)
Total cash flow from operations	$_____

10. What kind of activity is described by each of the events of the transactions below?

(a) Jones Co. buys a piece of equipment for $40,000.

[operating / investing / financing]

(b) Jones Co. borrows $50,000 from a bank, signing a long-term note payable.

[operating / investing / financing]

(c) Jones Co. pays $20,000 of its outstanding accounts payable.

[operating / investing / financing]

(d) Smith Corp. arranges $10,000 in new short-term borrowings from the bank.

[operating / investing / financing]

(e) Smith Corp. issues 1,000 of its common stock for $10 per share.

[operating / investing / financing]

(f) Smith Corp. sells one of the buildings it used for operations for $500,000.

[operating / investing / financing]

Answers for Post Test 9 are on page 38.

POST TEST 10

1. Use the following data:

Inventory	20	Sales revenue	100
Total current assets	100	Cost of sales	60
Total assets	220	Gross margin	40
Current liabilities	40	EBIT	30
Noncurrent liabilities	80	Net income	10
Equity	100		

(a) The current ratio was:

$$\frac{\quad\quad}{\quad\quad} = \underline{\quad\quad}$$

(b) The inventory turnover was:

$$\frac{\quad\quad}{\quad\quad} = \underline{\quad\quad} \text{ times}$$

(c) The profit margin percentage was:

$$\frac{\rule{3cm}{0.4pt}}{\rule{2cm}{0.4pt}} = \underline{\hspace{1cm}}\%$$

(d) The debt ratio (to the nearest percent) was:

$$\frac{\rule{3cm}{0.4pt}}{\rule{2cm}{0.4pt}} = \underline{\hspace{1cm}}\%$$

(e) The return on equity investment was:

$$\frac{\rule{3cm}{0.4pt}}{\rule{2cm}{0.4pt}} = \underline{\hspace{1cm}}\%$$

(f) The EBIT margin was:

$$\frac{\rule{3cm}{0.4pt}}{\rule{2cm}{0.4pt}} = \underline{\hspace{1cm}}\%$$

(g) The capital turnover (to one decimal place) was:

$$\frac{\rule{3cm}{0.4pt}}{\rule{2cm}{0.4pt}} = \underline{\hspace{1cm}}\text{times}$$

(h) The pretax return on permanent capital (to the nearest percent) was:

2. The pretax return on permanent capital can also be calculated by multiplying the c_____ t_____ by the _____ margin.

3. A company can decrease its equity by:
(a) . . . [increasing / decreasing] its assets.
(b) . . . [increasing / decreasing] its liabilities.

4. Liquidity means a company's ability to meet its _____ obligations.

5. Solvency means a company's ability to meet its _____-_____ obligations.

6. Accounting cannot provide a complete picture of the status or performance of an entity because:
(a) Accounting deals only with events that can be reported in m_____ terms.
(b) Financial statements report only p_____ events.
(c) Balance sheets do not show the f_____ v_____ of assets.
(d) The accountant and management have . . . [some latitude / no choice] in choosing among alternative ways of recording an event (e.g., LIFO, FIFO, or average cost).
(e) Accounting amounts are affected by e_____.

Answers for Post Test 10 are on pages 38 and 39.

POST TEST 11

1. Nonprofit entities have three basic financial statements:

_____ _____ _____ _____

_____ _____ _____

_____ _____ _____ _____

2. In a nonprofit organization the difference between revenues and expenses is called a _____.

3. The surplus is not always the appropriate measure of _____ in a nonprofit.

4. In many instances the m_____ and g_____ of nonprofit organizations are very different from for-profits. Therefore, different _____ _____ performance are required.

5. There are three types of net assets that must be reported on a nonprofit's statement of financial position:

_____ _____

_____ _____

_____

6. The classification of net assets depends on the intention of the _____.

7. The gains and losses on investments held by nonprofits must be reported as _____ in the current accounting period.

8. The cash or investment portion of a nonprofit's assets derived from donations is called an _____.

9. When restricted funds are used for their intended purpose, they show up on the financial statements as _____.

10. The reason that ROE may be an inappropriate measure of financial performance for a nonprofit organization is:

_____

_____

_____

Answers for Post Test 11 are on page 39.

Answers for Post Tests

ANSWERS FOR POST TEST 1

1. (a) assets

   (b) cash

   (c) liabilities

   (d) equity

2. liabilities

   equity

3. at a point in time

4. Assets = Liabilities + Equity

5. Dual-aspect concept

6. monetary amounts

7. money-measurement concept

8. no better or worse off; less; entity

9. entities; persons

10.

LEWIS CORPORATION

Balance Sheet as of December 31, 2001

Assets		Liabilities and Equity	
Cash	$12,000	Liabilities	$10,000
Other assets	25,000	Equity	27,000
Total	$37,000	Total	$37,000

11. entity; indefinitely

12. fair value; cost

13. Yes: (a), (e), (f)

   No: (b), (c), (d)

14. purchased

15. one year

16. one year

17. current; noncurrent

18. True; False

19. prepaid expense

20. property; plant

21. inventory; plant and property

22. receivable; payable

23. F (a, b, c, d, e) Note: All the statements are false. Assets must have been acquired at a measurable cost. Neither the amount reported as paid-in capital nor the amount of total equity has any necessary relation to fair value or what the entity is worth. Retained earnings is not cash; cash is an asset on the left-hand side of the balance sheet.

ANSWERS FOR POST TEST 2

1.

BROWN COMPANY

Balance Sheet as of January 31

Assets		Liabilities and Equity	
Cash	$11,500	Notes payable.........	$15,000
Accounts receivable..........	2,500	Paid-in capital	5,000
Inventory................	2,000	Retained earnings...	3,000
Automobile	7,000		
Total.................	$23,000	Total	$23,000

BROWN COMPANY

Income Statement for January

Revenue.......................................	$6,000
Expense	2,000
Income	$4,000

2. f

3. No; asset-measurement cost; fair value

ANSWERS FOR POST TEST 3

1. JOURNAL

March 5	Inventory	6,000	
	Cash		6,000

2. JOURNAL

March 10	Cash	6,000	
	Accounts Receivable	9,000	
	Revenues		15,000

3. JOURNAL

March 10	Expenses	8,000	
	Inventory		8,000

4. JOURNAL

March 31	Revenues	15,000	
	Retained earnings		15,000
March 31	Retained earnings	8,000	
	Expenses		8,000

5. No response

6.

Cash

Bal.	25,000	6,000
	6,000	
Bal.	25,000	

Accounts Receivable

Bal.	11,000	
	9,000	
Bal.	20,000	

Inventory

Bal.	40,000	8,000
	6,000	
Bal.	38,000	

Property and Plant

Bal.	30,000	

7.

Accounts Payable

	16,000 Bal.

Paid-in Capitol

	60,000 Bal.

Revenues

15,000	15,000

Expenses

8,000	8,000

Retained Earnings

8,000	30,000	Bal.
	15,000	
	37,000	Bal

8.

	Debits	Credits
Increases in asset accounts are	X	
Decreases in asset accounts are		X
Increases in liability accounts are		X
Decreases in liability accounts are	X	
Increases in equity accounts are		X
Decreases in equity accounts are	X	
Increases in revenue accounts are		X
Increases in expense accounts are	X	

9.

KAY COMPANY

Balance Sheet as of March 31

Assets		Liabilities and Equity	
Cash	$25,000	Accounts payable	$16,000
Accounts receivable	20,000	Paid-in capital	60,000
Inventory	38,000	Retained earnings	37,000
Property and plant	30,000		
Total	$113,000	Total	$113,000

10.

KAY COMPANY

Income Statement for March

Revenues	$15,000
Expenses	8,000
Income	$ 7,000

11. incorrect

12. retained earnings; cash

ANSWERS FOR POST TEST 4

1. (a) reasonably certain
(b) reasonably possible

2. (a) trivial matters
(b) important matters

3. one year; interim

4. equity; retained earnings

5. revenues; expenses; income

6. delivered

7. November

8. (a) Advances from customers (a liability)
(b) Revenue
(c) Accounts receivable (an asset)

9. (a) Accounts receivable
(b) Cash
(c) Advances from customers

10.

February	Cash	100	
	Advances from customers		100
March	Accounts receivable	500	
	Advances from customers	100	
	Revenue		600
March	Expenses	400	
	Inventory		400
April	Cash	500	
	Accounts receivable		500

11. (a) Revenue

(b) Allowance for doubtful accounts

(c) $198,000

(d) $598,000

12. (a) Allowance for doubtful accounts

(b) Accounts receivable

ANSWERS FOR POST TEST 5

1. acquired; consumed

2. expenditure; asset; expense

3. unexpired; expired

4. costs; expenses

5. (a) costs; delivered
(b) expenditures; operations
(c) losses

6. Prepaid; asset
Accrued; liability

7. $10,000

8. sales revenue; cost of sales

9. Gross margin
Sales revenue

10. net income (or income)

11. dividends

12. (d) = (c) + (a) − (b)

ANSWERS FOR POST TEST 6

1. Dr. Cash   800

   Cr. Revenue   800

Dr. Cost of Sales   600

   Cr. Inventory   600

2. each item

3. Cost of sales = beginning inventory + purchases
– ending inventory

4.

	Cost of Sales
(a) FIFO	$300
(b) LIFO	340
(c) Average cost	320

5. higher; lower

6. Dr. Cost of sales   1,000

   Cr. Inventory   1,000

7. Direct materials, direct labor, and overhead.

8. incurred

9. sold

10. Total production overhead costs
Total direct labor costs

11. $110 [= $50 + $40 + $20]

12. better; less; less

ANSWERS FOR POST TEST 7

1. all costs

2. five

3. is not; service life

4. (a) $18,000

    (b) 10

    (c) $1,800

    (d) Depreciation expense

           Accumulated depreciation

    (e) (1) Plant $20,000

        (2) Less accumulated

             depreciation 9,000

        (3) Book value $11,000

5. (a) zero

    (b) [x] (2) It will be reported as follows:

    Machine $20,000

       Accumulated depreciation 20,000

                  Book value 0

6. (a) gain; $3,000

    (b) Dr. Cash

         Cr. Gain on disposition (or sale) of assets

7.

	Example	Write-off process
Plant asset	machine, building	
Wasting asset	coal, oil, minerals	Depletion
Intangible asset	goodwill, trademark	Amortization

8. $400,000 (40,000 barrels @ $10 per barrel, not $50,000)

9. net amount; cost; accumulated depreciation; net amount

10. low; fairly

11. more; less; the same

12. reduces

13. $2,400,000

14. Deferred income tax; liability

ANSWERS FOR POST TEST 8

1. current assets; current liabilities

2. debt; equity

3. interest; principal; sometimes

4. paid-in capital; shareholders; retained earnings

5. Common stock   1,000

    Other paid-in capital   9,000

6. (a) $10

    (b) $30,000

    (c) can't tell (equity does not represent "worth")

    (d) can't tell (equity has no relation to cash)

    (e) at least $40,000 (it exceeds $40,000 by the amount of the dividends)

    (f) can't tell (equity does not show liquidation value)

7. issued; outstanding

8. treasury; 140,000

9. dividends; par value

10. decreases; does not change; increases

11. Yes No
Yes No
Higher Lower
Lower Higher

12. (a) 80 percent
(b) leveraged

13. parent; Able Company, Charlie Company; minority interest

14. $1,470,000 (= $1,000,000 – 10,000 + 500,000 – 20,000)

ANSWERS FOR POST TEST 9

1. required

2. accrual; cash

3. operating activities; investing activities; financing activities

4. increased

5. decreased

6. is not

7. was not

8. added to net income

9. 2,000
5,000
(3,000)
$54,000

10. investing (a, f)
financing (b, d, e)
operating (c)

ANSWERS FOR POST TEST 10

1. (a) $\dfrac{100}{40} = 2.5$

(b) $\dfrac{60}{20} = 3$ times

(c) $\dfrac{10}{100} = 10\%$

(d) $\dfrac{80}{180} = 44\%$

(e) $\dfrac{10}{100} = 10\%$

(f) $\dfrac{30}{100} = 30\%$

(g) $\dfrac{100}{180} = 0.6$ times

(h) $\dfrac{30}{180} = 17\%$

2. capital turnover; EBIT

3. (a) decreasing
(b) increasing

4. current

5. long-term debt

6. Any three of the following.

   (a) monetary

(b) past

(c) fair value

(d) some latitude

(e) estimates

ANSWERS FOR POST TEST 11

1. Statement of Financial Position

   Statement of Activities

   Statement of Cash Flows

2. surplus

3. performance

4. mission; goals; measures of

5. permanently restricted

   temporarily restricted

   unrestricted

6. donor

7. income

8. endowment

9. transfers

10. Nonprofit organizations do not have owners and hence, they don't have equity.

Glossary and Index

Note: The definitions here are brief. For a fuller discussion and examples, see the frames indicated. References are to parts and frames; e.g. 1:13–17 means part 1, frames 13–17.

Accelerated depreciation   A method of depreciation that charges off more of the original cost of a plant asset in the earlier years than in the later years of the asset's service life. Used mainly in calculating taxable income. **(7:36–38, 62–77)**

Account   A record in which the changes for a balance sheet or income statement item are recorded. **(3:1–2)**

Account payable   The amount that the entity owes to a supplier, not evidenced by a note. **(2:18–19)**

Account receivable   An amount that is owed to the business, usually as a result of the ordinary extension of credit to one of its customers. **(2:4)**

Accounting income   Income measured according to accounting principles. Contrast with **Taxable income**. **(7:38)**

Accounting period   The period of time over which an income statement summarizes the changes in equity. Usually the *official* period is one year, but income statements are also prepared for a shorter, or *interim*, period. **(4:3–5)**

Accrual accounting   Accounting for revenues in the period in which they are earned and for expenses in the period in which they are incurred. This is normal accounting practice. Cash accounting, which accounts only for cash receipts and payments, is usually not acceptable. **(4:6–17)**

Accrued expense   Another term for **Accrued liability**. Note that this is a liability account, not an expense account. **(5:35–39)**

Accrued liability   A liability that arises because an expense occurs in a period prior to the related cash payment. Example: accrued wages payable. **(5:37–39)**

Accrued pensions   The amount a company owes its employees for the benefits they accumulated under a pension plan. The liability is measured as the benefits accumulate. **(5:40–42)**

Accumulated depreciation   An account showing the total amount of an asset's depreciation that has been accumulated to date. It is subtracted from the cost of the asset; the difference is the asset's Book value. **(7:44–54)**

Additional paid-in capital   The amount paid by investors in excess of the par or stated value of the stock. **(8:26)**

Advances from customers   A liability account showing the amount due customers who have paid for goods or services in advance of their delivery. Sometimes called Deferred revenue, Precollected revenue, or Unearned revenue. **(4:44–51)**

Allowance for doubtful accounts   The amount of estimated bad debts that is included in accounts receivable. This amount is subtracted from accounts receivable on the balance sheet. **(4:65–71)**

Amortization   The process of writing off the cost of intangible assets. Sometimes used as a name for expensing the cost of all assets. **(7:68–70)**

Asset   A valuable item that is owned or controlled by the entity and that was acquired at a measurable cost. **(1:63–72)**

Asset-measurement concept   Accounting focuses on the fair value of monetary assets and on the cost of nonmonetary assets. **(1:44–57)**

Auditing   An examination of accounting records by independent, outside public accountants. **(10:6–10)**

Authorized stock   The total number of shares of stock that a corporation is permitted to issue. (The total number actually issued is usually a smaller amount.) **(8:27)**

Available for sale   The sum of beginning inventory and purchases during the period. **(6:13–15)**

Average-cost method   Finding cost of sales by taking the average cost per unit of the beginning inventory plus purchases. **(6:35–36)**

Bad debt   An account receivable that never will be collected. **(4:59–62)**

Bad debt expense   The estimated amount of bad debts applicable to an accounting period. **(4:58–71)**

Balance   The difference between the totals of the two sides of an account. An account has either a debit balance or a credit balance. (See **3:8, 63** for procedure for balancing an account.)

Balance sheet   A financial statement that reports the assets, liabilities, and equity of a company at one point in time. Assets are listed on the left and liabilities and equity on the right. (For balance sheet items, *see* 1:58–87.)

Benchmarking   Comparing an entity's performance against the performance of the company thought to be the best managed in the industry. **(10:15)**

Bond   A written promise to repay money furnished the business, with interest, at some future date, usually more than one year hence. **(8:8–16)**

Book value   The difference between the cost and the accumulated depreciation of a depreciable asset. **(7:46)**

Calendar year   The year that ends on the last day of the calendar, December 31. The accounting period for many entities is the calendar year, but some use the **Natural business year**. **(4:4–5)**

Capital   In general, the amount of funds supplied to an entity. **(8:1–6)** Also used as the name for **Paid-in capital** in a proprietorship or partnership.

Capital-intensive   Characterizes a company that has a large capital investment in relation to its sales revenue. **(10:63)**

Capital lease An item the entity controls by a lease agreement that extends over almost the whole life of the item. A capital lease is an asset. **(7:9–12)**

Capital stock A balance sheet account showing the amount that the shareholders contributed in exchange for stock. This plus retained earnings equals equity in a corporation. **(8:17–37)**

Capital turnover A ratio obtained by dividing annual sales by the amount of **permanent capital**. **(10:63–65)**

Capital utilization, tests of **(10:29–49)**

Cash The name for money, whether in currency or in a bank account. **(1:70–71)**

Cash flow statement A financial statement reporting the sources and uses of cash during an accounting period. **(Part 9)**

Cash-basis accounting An accounting system that does not use the accrual basis; it records only cash receipts and payments. Usually not an acceptable basis for accounting. **(4:10–15)**

Charge (verb) To debit an account.

Claim Amount owed to creditors or others who have provided money or have extended credit to a business. **(1:11–12)**

Closing entries Journal entries that transfer the balances in revenue and expense accounts for a period to retained earnings. **(3:51–62)**

Common stock Stock whose owners are not entitled to preferential treatment with regard to dividends or to the distribution of assets in the event of liquidation. **(3:25–30)** Its book value is not related to its market value. **(8:31–32)**

Comparisons, bases of Performance can be compared with past performance, with performance of other entities, or with a judgmental standard. (*See* **10:14–17**)

Concepts *See* **5:90–98** for a summary of accounting concepts.

Conservatism concept Recognize increases in equity only when they are reasonably certain; recognize decreases as soon as they are reasonably possible. **(4:18–22)**

Consolidated statements Financial statements prepared for a whole corporate family as an entity. The family consists of a **Parent** and its **Subsidiaries**. **(8:65–70)**

Contra-asset account An account whose balance is subtracted from that of the corresponding asset account. **(4:65)**

Conversion cost The labor and overhead costs of converting raw material into finished products. **(6:48)**

Cost A monetary measure of the amount of resources used for some purpose. (For product cost, *see* **6:54–63**. For acquisition cost, *see* **7:5–8**. *See also* **Period costs**.)

Cost accounting The process of identifying and accumulating manufacturing costs and assigning them to goods in the manufacturing process. **(6:53)**

Cost of goods sold Same as Cost of sales.

Cost of sales Cost of the same products whose revenues are included in sales revenue. **(Part 6)**

Credit (noun) The right-hand side of an account or an amount entered on the right-hand side of an account. Abbreviated as Cr. **(3:26–31)**

Credit (verb) To make an entry on the right-hand side of an account. Rules for debit and credit are summarized in **3:42**.

Creditor A person who lends money or extends credit to an entity. **(1:10–12)**

Current assets Cash and assets that are expected to be converted into cash or used up in the near future, usually within one year. **(2:1–9)**

Current liabilities Obligations that become due within a short period of time, usually one year. **(2:17–23)**

Current ratio The ratio obtained by dividing the total of the current assets by the total of the current liabilities. **(1:77–78; 10:40–41)**

Days' sales uncollected The number of days of sales that are tied up in accounts receivable as of the end of the accounting period. Sales per day is found by dividing annual credit sales by 365, and accounts receivable is divided by sales per days to find the days' receivables. **(4:74–77; 10:34)**

Debit (noun) The left-hand side of an account or an amount entered on the left-hand side of an account. Abbreviated as Dr. **(3:26–31)**

Debit (verb) To make an entry on the left-hand side of an account. Rules for debit and credit are summarized in **3:42**.

Debt capital The capital raised by the issuance of debt securities, usually bonds. **(8:7–9)** For differences between debt capital and equity capital. **(8:56–61)**

Debt ratio The ratio of debt capital to total permanent capital. **(8:62–64; 10:45–48)**

Deduction method Finding cost of sales by adding the beginning inventory and purchases and subtracting the ending inventory. **(6:9–19)**

Deferred income taxes The difference between the actual income tax for the period and income tax expense. **(7:38)**

Deferred revenue *See* **Advances from customers**.

Depletion The process of writing off the cost of a wasting asset, such as natural gas, coal, oil, or other minerals. **(7:62–66)**

Depreciable cost The difference between the cost of a plant asset and its estimated residual value. **(7:28)**

Depreciation expense The portion of the estimated net cost of plant assets (e.g., buildings, equipment) that becomes an expense in a given accounting period. **(5:34; 7:13–54)** (For accounting entries, *see* **7:39–54**.

Depreciation rate The percentage of the cost of an asset that is an expense each year. In the straight-line method, the rate is 1 divided by the service life. **(7:33–34)**

Derivative An instrument issued by a financial institution that promises to pay interest, for example, derived from underlying obligations such as mortgages. Some companies obtain funds by issuing such instruments backed by other instruments. Also, any type of transaction whose value depends, at least in part, upon the value of a related asset or liability. **(8:16)**

Direct labor or materials The labor or material that is used directly on a product. **(6:50–52)**

Disposition of plant, gain or loss on The difference between book value and the amount actually realized from a sale of a plant asset. **(7:55–57)**

Dividend The funds generated by profitable operations that are distributed to shareholders. Dividends are *not* an expense. **(5:76; 8:38–49)**

Double-entry system A characteristic of accounting in which each transaction recorded causes at least two changes in the accounts.

Dual-aspect concept The total assets of an entity always are equal to its total liabilities and equity. **(1:16–26)**

Earnings Another term for **Net income**. **(2:81)**

Earnings before interest and taxes (EBIT) An amount used in calculating return on permanent capital. **(10:58–60)**

Earnings per share A ratio obtained by dividing the total earnings for a given period by the number of shares of common stock outstanding. **(10:50)**

EBIT margin Earnings before interest and income taxes as a percentage of sales revenue. **(10:59)**

Entity A business or other organization for which a set of accounts is kept. **(1:2, 3)**

Entity concept Accounts are kept for entities, rather than for the persons who own, operate, or are otherwise associated with those entities. **(1:34–39)**

Entry The accounting record made for a single transaction. **(3:44–45)**

Equation, fundamental accounting Assets = Liabilities + Equity. **(1:21–26)**

Equity Capital supplied by (1) equity investors and (2) the entity's retained earnings. Also, claims against the entity by equity investors. **(1:79–87; 8:17–22)**

Equity capital The capital supplied by owners, who are called equity investors. **(8:17–20)** For differences between debt capital and equity capital, *see* **8:50–61**.

Expenditure The decrease in an asset or increase in a liability associated with the acquisition of goods or services. Do not confuse with **Expense**, which represents the use of goods and services and which may occur after the expenditure. **(5:3–14)**

Expense A decrease in equity resulting from operations during an accounting period; that is, resources used up or consumed during an accounting period. **(2:73)** Example: wage expense. **(5:3–14)** For assets that will become expenses, *see* **5:17, 24–34**; for expenses that create liabilities, *see* **5:35–39**.

Expensing The process of charging the cost of an asset to expense.

Expired cost Another name for Expense. **(5:15–18)**

External basis of comparison Comparing an entity's performance with the performance of other entities. **(10:15)**

Face amount The total amount of a loan that must be repaid, specified on the face of a bond. **(8:9)**

Fair value The amount for which an asset can be sold in the marketplace. **(1:44–57)**

FIFO (first-in, first-out) method Finding cost of sales on the assumption that the oldest goods (those first in) were the first to be sold (first out). **(6:27–31)**

Financial statements *See* the three required financial statements: balance sheet, income statement, statement of cash flows.

Fiscal year *See* **Natural business year**.

Fixed assets Tangible, **noncurrent assets (7:3)**

Free cash flow The amount remaining after special needs for cash in the coming period is subtracted from the cash flow expected from operating activities. (See note after **9-63**)

Fringe benefits Benefits, principally monetary, beyond wages; owed to an employee because of his or her service to the company. **(5:40–44)**

Gain (or loss) on disposition of plant *See* **7:55–57**.

Going-concern concept Accounting assumes that an entity will continue to operate indefinitely. **(1:40–43)**

Goods available for sale The sum of the beginning inventory plus purchases during the period. **(6:13–15)**

Goodwill An intangible asset; the amount paid in excess of the value of a company's identifiable net assets, representing an amount paid for a favorable location or reputation. Goodwill is an asset only if it was purchased. **(2:16)**

Gross margin The difference between sales revenue and cost of sales. **(5:71)**

Gross margin percentage Gross margin as a percentage of sales revenue. **(5:87–88; 10:22–25)**

Historic cost concept *See* **Cost concept**.

Historical basis of comparison Comparing an entity's performance with its own performance in the past. **(10:14)**

Income The amount by which equity increased as a result of operations during a period of time. **(2:67–71, 2:81)**

Income statement A statement of revenues and expenses, and the difference between them, for an accounting period; a flow report. It explains the changes in equity associated with operations of the period. **(2:68–81; 5:67–68)**

Income tax A tax levied as a percentage of taxable income. *See* **Taxable income**.

Intangible asset An asset that has no physical substance, such as goodwill or the protection provided by an insurance policy. **(2:14–16, 56; 5:26–30; 7:67–70)**

Interest The amount paid for the use of money. A loan requires payment of both interest and **Principal**. **(8:12–16)**

Interest expense   The entity's cost of using borrowed funds during an accounting period. **(8:12–16)**

Interest revenue   Revenue earned from permitting someone to use the entity's money. Revenue from the "rental" of money. Often but erroneously called interest income. **(4:54)**

Interim statements   Financial statements prepared for a period shorter than one year, such as a month or a quarter. **(4:4)**

Intrafamily transactions   Transactions between the corporations in a consolidated family. These transactions are eliminated in preparing consolidated financial statements. **(8:69)**

Inventory (noun)   Goods being held for sale, and material and partially finished products that will be sold upon completion. **(2:45)** For inventory valuation methods, *see* **Part 6.**

Inventory (verb)   To conduct a physical observation and count of inventory. **(6:16–17)**

Inventory turnover   A ratio that shows how many times inventory was totally replaced during the year; calculated by dividing the average inventory into cost of sales. **(6:65–68; 10:38)**

Investments   Securities that are held for a relatively long period of time and are purchased for reasons other than the temporary use of excess cash. They are noncurrent assets.

Issued stock   The shares of stock that have been issued. Issued stock less **Treasury stock** equals **Outstanding stock**. **(9:29)** Contrast with **Authorized stock.**

Journal   A record in which transactions are recorded in chronological order. It shows the accounts to be debited or credited and the amount of each debit and credit. Transactions are **Posted** to the **ledger**. **(3:44)**

Judgmental basis of comparison   Comparing an entity's performance with our personal judgment. **(10:16)**

Land, life of   *See* 7:13.

Lease   An agreement under which the owner of property permits someone else to use it. The owner is the *lessor*. The user is the *lessee*. **(7:9–12)**

Ledger   A group of accounts. Entries are posted to the ledger from the journal. **(3:43)**

Leverage   The proportion of **debt capital** to total **permanent capital**. A company that obtains a high proportion of its permanent capital from debt is said to be *highly leveraged*. **(8:50–64)**

Liability   The equity or claim of a creditor. **(1:10; 1:73–76)**

LIFO (last-in, first-out) method   Finding cost of sales on the assumption that the goods most recently purchased (last in) were the first to be sold (first out). **(6:32–34)**

Limitations on financial statement analysis   **(10:1–5)**

Liquidity   An entity's ability to meet its current obligations. Often measured by the current ratio. **(11:71)**

Losses   Expenses resulting from assets whose future benefit has expired during a period, for example, from fire or theft, and liabilities occurring in a period, for example, from lawsuits. **(5:50–52)** *See also* **Gain (or loss).**

Manufacturing company   A company that converts raw materials into finished, salable products and then sells these products. **(6:46–49)** For accounting for inventory in a manufacturing company, *see* 6:46–63.

Manufacturing overhead   *See* **Production overhead cost.**

Marketable securities   Securities that are expected to be converted into cash within a year; a current asset. **(2:3, 2:14)**

Matching concept   Costs that are associated with the revenues of a period are expenses of that period. **(5:19–23).**

Materiality concept   Disregard trivial matters, but disclose all important matters. **(4:23–30)**

Measurable cost   An item whose amount is known, usually because the item was acquired from an outside party. **(1:67)**

Merchandising company   A company that sells goods that it has acquired from other businesses; for example, a retail store or a wholesaler. **(6:47–48)**

Minority interest   The equity of those shareholders in a subsidiary other than the equity of the parent. Reported as an equity item on the consolidated balance sheet. **(8:75)**

Monetary assets   Cash and promises by an outside party to pay the entity a specified amount of money. **(4:72–73)**

Money-measurement concept   Accounting records report only facts that can be expressed in monetary amounts. Accounting therefore does not give a complete record of an entity. **(1:27–33)**

Mortgage   A pledge of real estate as security for a loan. **(2:57)**

Mortgage payable   The liability for a loan that is secured by a mortgage. **(2:57)**

Natural business year   A year that ends on the day that activities are at a relatively low level. For some entities, the accounting period is the natural business year, rather than the calendar year. **(4:5)** Also called the **fiscal year.**

Net   The amount remaining after something has been subtracted from a gross amount. Example: accounts receivable, net. **(4:68)**

Net Assets   In a nonprofit organization, the portion of the balance sheet occupied by equity in a for-profit organization. Alternatively, Assets − Liabilities. Net assets may be unrestricted, temporarily restricted or permanently restricted. **(11:15–24)**

Net income   The amount by which total revenues exceed total expenses for an account period; the "bottom line." **(5:75)**

Net income percentage   Net income expressed as a percentage of sales revenue. **(5:89)**

Net loss   The amount by which total expenses exceed total revenues in an accounting period; negative net income. **(5:75)**

Net worth   Another (but misleading) name for equity. **(8:43)**

Nonbusiness organizations Municipalities, hospitals, religious organizations, and other organizations that are not operated for the purpose of earning a profit. *See note after* **1:39**.

Noncurrent asset An asset that is expected to be of use to the entity for longer than one year. **(2:10–16)**

Noncurrent liability A claim that does not fall due within one year. Similar to **Debt capital**. **(2:24)**

Nonprofit or not-for-profit An entity with no ownership or shareholders. The regulations to determine nonprofit status vary from state to state. **(11:2–4)**

No-par-value stock Common stock that does not have a par value. It is recorded at its **Stated value**. **(8:26)**

Note A written promise to pay. **(2:37)**

Note payable A liability evidenced by a written promise to pay. **(2:37)**

Obsolescence A loss in the usefulness of an asset because of the development of improved equipment, changes in style, or other causes not related to the physical condition of the asset. It is one cause of depreciation; the other cause is wearing out. **(7:20)**

Opinion or Opinion letter The report in which the auditor gives his or her opinion as to the fairness of the financial statements. **(10:6–10)**

Other post-employment benefits (OPEB) Health care or other fringe benefits, besides pensions, owed to an employee after his or her employment ends. **(5:43–44)**

Outstanding stock Shares of stock held by investors. Consists of **Issued stock** less **Treasury stock**. **(8:28)**

Overhead *See* **Production overhead cost**.

Overhead rate A rate used to allocate overhead costs to products. **(6:59–63)**

Owners' equity The claims of owners against the assets of a business. In a corporation, owners' equity consists of capital stock plus retained earnings. **(2:25–26)**

Package of accounting reports *See* **Report package**.

Paid-in capital The amount paid by investors in exchange for stock. The amount in excess of the stock's par or stated value is called **Additional paid-in capital**. **(1:79–81; 2:25; 8:24)**

Par value The specific amount printed on the face of some stock certificates. No longer significant in accounting. **(9:23)**

Parent A corporation that controls one or more other corporations because it owns more than 50 percent of their stock. The controlled corporations are its **Subsidiaries**. **(9:65)**

Partnership An unincorporated business with two or more owners. **(1:39)**

Patent A grant that gives an inventor the exclusive right, for 17 years, to produce and sell an invention. **(2:15)**

Percentage A number obtained by dividing one number by another (which is the base, or 100 percent), and multiplying by 100. Income statement items are often expressed as percentages of sales revenue.

Performance, measures of For overall measures of performance, *see* **10:11–20**; for tests of capital utilization, *see* **10:29–49**; for other measures, *see* **10:50–65; 11:64**.

Period costs Costs associated with general sales and administrative activities. Contrast with **Product costs**. **(6:54–58)**

Permanent account An account for a balance sheet item, so called because it is not closed at the end of the accounting period. Contrast with **Temporary account**. **(3:62)**

Permanent capital The sum of noncurrent liabilities and equity. **(8:6)**

Permanently restricted net assets In a nonprofit organization, assets donated for specific purposes which cannot be used in other ways. **(11:16, 18)**

Perpetual inventory A record of the cost of each item in inventory showing the quantity and the cost of receipts, issues, and the amount on hand, updated nearly simultaneously for each day's activity. **(6:5–6)**

Physical inventory The amount of inventory currently on hand, obtained by making a physical count. **(6:16–17)**

Plant assets All tangible, noncurrent assets except land. **(2:10; 7:3–4)** For acquisition of plant assets, see **7:5–8**. For sale of plant assets, *see* **7:55–57**.

Posting The process of transferring transactions from the **journal** to the **ledger**. **(3:49, 50)**

Precollected revenue *See* **Advances from customers**.

Preferred stock Stock whose owners have a preferential claim over common stockholders for dividends and for assets in the event of liquidation. **(8:34–37)**

Prepaid expenses The general name for intangible assets that will become expenses in future periods when the services they represent are used up. Example: prepaid insurance. **(2:9; 5:27–31)**

Price-earnings ratio A ratio obtained by dividing the average market price of the stock by the earnings per share. **(10:53–55)**

Principal The amount that must be repaid on a loan. The total repayment consists of principal plus **Interest**. **(8:12)**

Product Goods or services sold or to be sold. (Sometimes refers only to tangible goods.)

Product costs The direct materials, direct labor, and production overhead costs of a product. Contrast with **Period costs**. **(6:54–58)**

Production overhead cost Product costs other than direct materials and direct labor. Includes, for example, supervision, building maintenance, and power. **(6:59–63)** *See also* **Overhead rate**.

Profit Another name for **Income**. **(2:81)**

Profit and loss statement Another name for **Income statement**. **(5:67–68)**

Profit margin percentage Net income divided by sales revenue. **(10:26)**

Proprietorship An unincorporated business with a single owner. **(1:38; 2:32)**

Ratio The result of dividing one number by another. *See,* for example, **Current ratio**.

Realization concept Revenue is recognized when goods or services are delivered, in an amount that is reasonably certain to be realized. **(4:31–38)**

Reasonably certain A criterion for deciding on the amount to be entered for an asset or liability account. **(4:59)**

Recognition The act of recording a revenue or expense item as being applicable to a given accounting period. Revenue recognition is governed by the **realization concept**. **(4:31–57)**

Rental revenue Revenue earned from permitting someone to use a building or other property. **(4:53–55)**

Report, Auditors' *See* **Opinion**.

Report package Consists of a balance sheet for the beginning and end of the accounting period and an income statement for the accounting period. **(5:79–82)**

Residual claim The claim of equity investors. **(1:15)**

Residual value The amount for which a company expects to be able to sell a plant asset for at the end of its service life. **(7:25–26)**

Retained earnings The increase in equity that has resulted from the operations of the entity. It is an equity item, not an asset. **(1:83–84; 5:79–85; 8:38–44)**

Return on equity (ROE) A ratio obtained by dividing net income by the amount of equity. **(10:11–21)**

Return on investment (ROI) Earnings before interest and taxes divided by noncurrent liabilities plus equity. (Some people calculate it in other ways.) **(10:56–61)**

Return on permanent capital Another name for **return on investment**. **(10:56–61)**

Revenue The increase in owners' equity resulting from operations during a period of time, usually from the sale of goods or services. **(2:72, 74)** For measuring the amount of revenue, *see* **4:58–71**.

Sales income Sometimes used to mean **Sales revenue**; a misleading term because income is the difference between sales revenue and expenses.

Sales revenue Revenue from the delivery of goods or services. **(4:37)**

Security An instrument such as a stock or bond. Securities give the entity that owns them valuable rights from the entity that issued them. **(2:2–3)**

Service An intangible product. Examples are personal services, rent, and insurance protection. **(4:52–55)**

Service life The period of time over which an asset is estimated to be of service to the entity. **(7:16–17, 21)**

Service revenue Revenue from the performance of services. **(4:52–55)**

Shareholder equity The equity section of a corporation's balance sheet. **(8:21)** Also called stockholder equity. *See also* **Equity**.

Shareholders The owners of a corporation. Also referred to as stockholders. **(8:21)**

Shrinkages Goods that have been stolen or spoiled and hence are no longer in inventory. **(6:18)**

Sole proprietorship *See* **Proprietorship**.

Solvency An entity's ability to meet its long-term obligations. Often measured by the **Debt ratio**. **(10:72)**

Specific identification method A way of calculating cost of sales by keeping track of the specific item (e.g., an automobile) sold. **(6:2)**

Stated value The amount at which **no-par-value stock** is reported on the balance sheet, as voted by the directors. **(8:26)**

Statement of activities In a nonprofit organization, the statement of revenues and expenses, or the statement which describes the change in net assets. **(11:8, 10)**

Statement of financial position Another name for a **Balance sheet**. **(11:9)**

Stock *See* **Capital stock, common stock, preferred stock**.

Stock dividend A dividend consisting of shares of stock in the corporation. **(8:47–49)**

Stock split An exchange of the number of shares of stock outstanding for a substantially larger number. **(8:48–50)**

Stockholders *See* **Shareholders**.

Straight-line depreciation A depreciation method that charges off an equal fraction of the estimated **depreciable cost** of a plant asset over each year of its service life. **(7:31–35)**

Subsidiary A corporation that is controlled by another corporation, Ω the **parent**, which owns more than 50 percent of its stock. **(8:65)**

Surplus In a nonprofit organization, the equivalent of profit, income, or earnings. **(11:5, 7)**

T-account The simplest version of an account. **(3:2–6)**

Tangible assets Assets that can be touched; they have physical substance. Noncurrent tangible assets are often referred to as property, plant, and equipment. **(2:10)**

Tax accounting principles (See **7:38**.)

Tax depreciation The depreciation used in calculating taxable income. **(7:38)**

Taxable income The amount of income subject to income tax, computed according to the rules of the Internal Revenue Service. For difference between taxable income and accounting income and the treatment of depreciation, see **8:38**.

Temporarily restricted net assets In a nonprofit organization, assets donated for specific purposes in a designated accounting period. **(11:16–17)**

Temporary account   A revenue or expense account. A temporary account is closed at the end of each accounting period. Contrast with **Permanent account**. (3:62)

Trademark   A distinctive name for a manufactured good or a service. (2:15)

Transaction   An event that is recorded in the accounting records; it always has at least two elements. (2:42–44)

Transfer   In a nonprofit organization, as funds are used for their intended purposes they are transferred from temporarily restricted funds to the unrestricted category on the statement of activities. (11:46–58)

Treasury stock   Previously issued stock that has been bought back by the corporation. (8:28)

Unearned revenue   *See* **Advances from customers**.

Unexpired cost   The cost of assets on hand now that will be consumed in future accounting periods. (5:15–18)

Units-of-production method   A depreciation method. A cost per unit of production is calculated, and depreciation expense for a year is found by multiplying this unit cost by the number of units that the asset produced in that year. (7:30)

Unrealized gain   Gains on invested funds, whether such investments are sold for cash or held for the future by an organization. (11:39–40, 42)

Unrestricted Activities   In a nonprofit organization, those activities reported on the statement of activities matched with unrestricted revenues. (11:36)

Unrestricted net assets   In a nonprofit organization, net assets that result from profitable operating activities or from donations with no restrictions. (11:16, 19, 23)

Wasting assets   Natural resources, such as coal, oil, and other minerals. The process of charging wasting assets to expense is called depletion. (7:62)

Working capital   The difference between current assets and current liabilities. (8:4)

Write down   To reduce the cost of an item, especially inventory, to its market value. (6:44)

Write-off of bad debt   To remove a bad debt from Accounts Receivable. (4:69–71)